WHAT THINK YE OF CHRIST?

WHOSE SON IS HE?

BY

HENRY CLAY MORRISON

First Fruits Press
Wilmore, Kentucky
c2013

ISBN: 9781621711315 (Print), 9781621711322 (Digital)

What Think ye of Christ? Whose Son is He?
A Sermon by Henry Clay Morrison
First Fruits Press, © 2013
Previously published by the Pentecostal Publishing Company, circa 1920

Digital version at
http://place.asburyseminary.edu/firstfruitsheritagematerial/70/

Morrison, H. C. (Henry Clay), 1857-1942.
What think ye of Christ? Whose son is He? : a sermon / by H.C. Morrison.
    28 p. ; 21 cm.
    Wilmore, Ky. : First Fruits Press, c2013.
    Reprint. Previously published: Louisville, Ky. : Pentecostal Pub. Co., [192-?].
    ISBN: 9781621711315 (pbk.)
    1. Jesus Christ -- Person and offices -- Sermons. 2. Bible. Matthew XXII, 42 -- Sermons. 3. Methodist Church -- Sermons. 4. Sermons, American. I. Title. II. Whose son is He?
BS2575 .M6 2013

Cover design by Haley Hill

asburyseminary.edu
800.2ASBURY
204 North Lexington Avenue
Wilmore, Kentucky 40390

First Fruits
THE ACADEMIC OPEN PRESS OF ASBURY SEMINARY

BOOKS BY HENRY CLAY MORRISON

The Two Lawyers
The Christ of the Gospels
Sermons for the Times
Lectures on Prophecy
The Second Coming of Christ
Romanism and Ruin
The Optimism of Pre-millennialism
Remarkable Conversions
  Interesting Incidents and
  Striking Illustrations
The Confessions of a Backslider
Crossing the Deadline
The Baptism With the Holy Ghost
The Pearl of Greatest Price
Will a Man Rob God?

What Think Ye of Christ? Whose Son is He?

SERMON
BY
REV. H. C. MORRISON, D. D,

※

PENTECOSTAL PUBLISHING COMPANY
Louisville, Kentucky.

WHAT THINK YE OF CHRIST?
WHOSE SON IS HE?
Matt. 22:42.

The chapter in the Gospel of Matthew from which we take our text, begins with that very interesting parable in which the Lord likens the kingdom of heaven to a certain king who made a marriage for his son. In this parable Jesus gives a very severe rebuke to the Jews. He tells how the king sent forth his servants to notify those who were bidden, that full preparation had been made for the marriage and the feast; but instead of coming to the marriage, they went their way, "One to his farm, and another to his merchandise." Others, however, "took his servants, entreated them spitefully, and slew them."

The king in indignation, sent his army and destroyed those persons who were so cordially invited to the marriage feast, and burned up their city. He then sent out his servants into the highways and gathered together both bad and good.

Dull as the Jews seemed to be in receiving any sort of spiritual knowledge of the teachings of Jesus, they did have

3

enough comprehension to apply something of this remarkable illustration to themselves. Evidently, our Lord spoke this parable as a prophecy of the judgments that would come upon the Jews, and the sending of the gospel to the Gentile world. It is common, when men are rebuked for their sins, if they will not forsake them, to become angry with the messenger of the Lord. It was so in this case, and at once, "the Pharisees took counsel how they might entangle him in his talk."

They sent to him a group made up of their own sect with a group of Herodians, taxgatherers, and asked him if it were lawful to pay tribute to Cæsar. They were eager to bring Christ into conflict with the Roman Government, and by this means to secure his death. Examining the coin and asking them whose superscription it bore, they answered, "Cæsar's." His answer was, "Render therefore unto Cæsar the things which are Cæsar's, and unto God the things which are God's." They were completely confounded and left the Lord.

In this answer Jesus turns a flood of light on practical living; our duty to human government, which must be met if we would be good citizens and true disciples of his. No man can be right with God and wrong with his fellow-men. The tax-collector must have his dues as well as God must have his tithes and offerings.

The Sadducees, who claimed that there was no resurrection of the dead, came to Jesus with a remarkable story of a certain woman who had married seven brothers; the first dying, according to the Mosaic law, she marries the second to raise up seed for his brother. He dies, and this marrying goes on until the seventh brother marries the woman and dies. They tell the Lord, "and last of all, the woman died also." We are not surprised that the woman died; she must have worked herself to death preparing for weddings and attending funerals. Our judgment is, it was a made-up case to meet the situation. We have noticed that men who oppose Jesus Christ have but little regard for the truth.

But having stated this remarkable case, they then demanded to know, "Therefore in the resurrection whose wife shall she be of the seven? For they all had her." This gave Jesus an opportunity to turn some very interesting light into the final hereafter of the human race. He says, "For in the resurrection they neither marry, nor are given in marriage, but are as the angels of God in heaven." He then assures them that God is not the God of the dead, but of the living, and that Abraham, Isaac and Jacob, their great patriarchs, are still alive, notwithstanding they had passed behind the curtain of physical death.

Then we have a lawyer of the Pharisees coming to Christ and asking him, "Which is the great commandment of the law?" In his answer Jesus lifts up a torch of light which has not, and cannot, be extinguished. "Thou shalt love the Lord thy God with all thy heart, and with all thy soul, and with all thy mind. This is the first and great commandment. And the second is like unto this, thou shalt love thy neighbor as thyself. On these two commandments hang all the law and the prophets." So illuminating and powerful an answer no doubt produced a silence, and it is at this moment that Jesus propounds to them the question which we have taken for our text: "What think ye of Christ? Whose son is he?"

You notice that he did not ask them,

"Who am I? Whom do you suppose me to be?" But what about the Christ your prophets have promised you? The great Redeemer of Israel whom you are awaiting and expecting? Whose son is this Christ of promise? At once they answered, "He is the son of David." The Lord then gives them a quotation from the Old Testament Scriptures in which David calls the Christ "His Lord." And says, "If David then called him Lord, how is he his son?"

Our Lord was showing them that, while he was typically the son of David, in fact, he was the eternal Son of God. These answers were so ready, so clear, so comprehensive and illuminating, that his enemies were confounded. The record tells us, "And no man was able to answer him a word, neither durst any man from that day forth ask him any more questions."

The question which our Lord put to his enemies on the occasion of which we have spoken, has ever been a vital question. It is especially so today, when from so many quarters vigorous attacks are being made upon his Deity. Not only are these attacks being made by atheists, who would, if possible, destroy and sweep out of the thought and belief of mankind the very existence of God himself, along with the manifestation of himself in Christ; but in many instances most dangerous skeptics in the pulpits of our country are attacking the Deity of our Lord. They are willing to agree that Jesus of Nazareth was a most extraordinary and superior man; that he was a worthy pattern for all men to seek to emulate, but that he was not, in any peculiar sense, the Son of God. This teaching is having a most baneful effect, it is destructive to all evangelical faith and movement. The results may be noted in the reckless living, the disregard of human life, and the increase of lawlessness and wickedness of every kind.

In view of these facts, the question contained in the text presents itself for most serious consideration. It is a question which each individual must face and answer for him or herself. No one can afford to be indifferent, or cast aside and neglect to ponder deeply this question—"What think ye of Christ? Whose son is he?"

Once Christ stood silently before Pilate awaiting his decision and pronouncement which had far more to do with Pilate than it had to do with

Christ. Christ had come into the world
to live, to teach, and to die for the redemption of a lost race. This was the
divine appointment from the Father.
Pilate could neither help nor hinder the
eternal plan and purposes of a God who
so loved the world that he gave his only
begotten Son to suffer death for its redemption; but Pilate could render a decision which would fix his own destiny.
Now Jesus stands before a generation of
human beings awaiting their decision,
the decision of each individual; and the
decision with reference to who he is,
and what he can do, will fix the destiny
of the individual. The weal or woe of
every intelligent human being rests upon what that being "thinks of Christ."

Jesus Christ has come to have powerful influence in the world. The sinless-
ness of his character, the faultlessness
of his conduct, the sublimity of the
principles he enunciated, the unselfish-
ness of his love and the patient forgiveness with which he suffered, has made
him the first and highest of all beings
who have ever lived and walked in human form upon the earth. Christ's life
and teachings have, in a most wonderful way, affected architecture, art and
literature. His spirit has permeated, to

some extent, in fact, in a marvelous way, all civil government, social and commercial life. Jesus is the most familiar name in all history; his sayings are repeated in the courts of the world, in the senates of wisest men, in the cabinets that gather for the forming of thought, the making of laws, and the administration of governments; about the campfires of the armies of the world men talk in subdued tones of the life and teachings of Christ. His life and the precepts and wisdom which fell from his lips are thrilling the human race with new conceptions of duty and happiness, and the uplift of all the vast multitudes of mankind to a better and a higher life.

Scholarly and thoughtful men who have not accepted Christ as the Son of God and Redeemer of mankind, after searching as deeply as the mere human mind, unilluminated by the Holy Spirit, could penetrate, have paid highest tribute to the character of Jesus. The historian, Lecky, who was a rationalist, says, "In the character and example of Christ is an enduring principle of regeneration." It is not to be supposed that this brilliant skeptic was at all thinking of the teaching of Christ when he said, "Ye must be born again." But he is evidently expressing the belief that in the character and example of Christ there were underlying principles and teaching which, if followed, would lift the entire race on to a high plane of peace and good will, and an altruistic spirit among men everywhere.

Renan, the French infidel, says, "The person of Jesus is at the highest summit of human greatness." He did not accept Jesus Christ as a divine person coming down from heaven to save a lost world, but he did, because of the purity of his character and the sublimity of his thought and teaching, lift him high above all other men of all ages, and place him at the head of the column of all philosophers, statesmen, philanthropists, and military chieftains.

John Stuart Mill, philosopher and agnostic, says of Jesus: "Everything which is excellent in ethics may be brought within the sayings of Christ without doing violence to the language. He is the ideal representative and guide to humanity." Mill is looked upon as one of our greatest philosophers. He has no faith or trust in Christ as a personal Saviour, but he studies his life;

he examines into his character; he ponders his teaching and he is forced to the conclusion that Jesus Christ "Is the ideal representative and guide to humanity."

We have quoted these selections from profound thinkers who are not Christian men, who do not believe in the Deity and saving power of our Lord, but who have deeply pondered his life, character and teaching and who, in their thought, believe him to be the highest, the greatest, and the best man who ever lived and wrought among his fellowbeings.

Let us now turn to an entirely different order of witnesses. Matthew, in his record of the gospel, the life and teachings of Jesus, tells us that an angel announced to the pure Virgin Mary the conception, birth and coming of our Lord. He tells us that he was begotten of the Holy Ghost; that in this miraculous way the eternal Son of God took upon himself the form of a man. Matthew says that the annunciation Angel said to Mary, "Thou shalt call his name JESUS: for he shall save his people from their sins."

St. Luke gives a more lengthy and graphic account of the interesting

events which attended the annunciation, and birth of Christ, and the sing-
ing hosts from heaven, the worshipping
shepherds, and the coming of the ador-
ing wise men. In Luke we read: "And
the angel said unto her, fear not,
Mary; for thou hast found favor with
God. And, behold, thou shalt conceive
in thy womb, and bring forth a son, and
shalt call his name JESUS. He shall
be great, and shall be called the Son of
the Highest: and the Lord God shall
give unto him the throne of his father
David: and he shall reign over the
house of Jacob forever; and of his kingdom there shall be no end."

It would seem impossible to ignore
and put aside these records of Matthew
and Luke, without putting aside their
entire gospels which contain these records. If these statements with reference to the birth of our Lord are not
trustworthy, how can we accept any
other part of their writings as trustworthy? It would seem the only reasonable and logical thing to do, is to
either accept these records of the birth
and coming of Jesus Christ into the
world, or to reject entirely, the gospels
of Matthew and Luke. This we cannot,
and will not do. We will, without hesi-

tation, accept as inspired truth and divinely authenticated history, the writings of Matthew and Luke with reference to the manner of the coming of our Lord Jesus Christ—God manifest in the flesh—into our world.

Some modernists who are seeking to rob the Lord Jesus of his Godhead, have boasted that neither John or St. Paul has ever written a hint with regard to the virgin birth or Godhead of Christ. We shall let John and St. Paul speak for themselves. Take the first chapter of the gospel of John, commencing with the first verse, we read: "In the beginning was the Word, and the word was with God, and the Word was God. The same was in the beginning with God. All things were made by him: and without him was not anything made that was made. In him was life; and the life was the light of men." Now read the fourteenth verse of this same chapter. "And the Word was made flesh, and dwelt among us, and we beheld his glory, the glory as of the ONLY BEGOTTEN OF THE FATHER, full of grace and truth."

Notice here that John says plainly and positively, that Jesus Christ was the "only begotten of the Father." The simplest of minds will understand that John was not referring to Joseph as the father of Christ, but to the eternal God. John's language in the beginning of the chapter, will easily bear this translation: "In the beginning was the Christ, and the Christ was with God, and the Christ was God. The same was in the beginning with God. All things were made by Christ; and without Christ was not anything made that was made. In Christ was life, and the life was the light of men. . . . And the Christ was made flesh, and dwelt among us, and we beheld the glory of Christ, the glory as of the only begotten of the Father, full of grace and truth." It is well understood by all Bible readers, that the WORD used by John in these scriptures refers to the Lord Jesus Christ. So our translation is perfectly safe and harmonizes with all New Testament teaching with regard to the person of our blessed Lord and Saviour.

With these clear statements from John the beloved, it would seem that no one, except those who are blinded with unbelief, could dare make the statement that there is not a hint in the writings of John with reference to the

Godhead of Christ. No one living on the earth during the ministry of our Lord in the flesh, knew him more intimately, loved him more devoutly, than John, and no one knew all of the miraculous circumstances with reference to his birth and ministry more minutely than John; and when John wrote what we have just quoted, he knew perfectly that he was in no sense the son of Joseph the carpenter. John goes back of all mere human beings and declares that, "In the beginning was the Christ, and Christ was with God, and the Christ was God." It is utterly stupid to suggest that John knew and wrote nothing about the Deity and virgin birth of our Lord. John knew what Matthew and Luke had written, and in the beginning of his beautiful and wonderful gospel he places his endorsement upon what they had written, and declares that Jesus Christ was God manifest in the flesh.

We shall now let the Apostle Paul speak for himself with reference to who Jesus was. Remember that Paul and St. Luke lived, traveled, worshipped and witnessed together, and that Paul knew exactly what Luke believed and taught with reference to our Christ's coming into the world. Knowing Paul, as we do, from his writings, it is manifest to every one, if he had not accepted Luke's teaching with reference to the virgin birth and Godhead of Jesus, he would not have hesitated to combat the teachings of Matthew and Luke. But with a perfect understanding of their faith and teaching he follows up with the following remarkable contribution. Speaking of Jesus, he says in the first chapter of his epistle to the Colossians 13:22: "Who hath delivered us from the power of darkness, and hath translated us into the kingdom of his dear Son: In whom we have redemption through his blood, even the forgiveness of sins: Who is the image of the invisible God, the firstborn of every creature: For by him were all things created, that are in heaven, and that are in earth, visible and invisible, whether they be thrones, or dominions, or principalities, or powers: all things were created by him, and for him: And he is before all things, and by him all things consist. And he is the head of the body, the church: who is the beginning, the firstborn from the dead; that in all things he might have the pre-eminence. For it pleased the Father that in him should all fulness dwell; and having made peace through the blood of his cross, by him to reconcile all things unto himself; by him, I say, whether they be things in earth, or things in heaven. And you, that were sometime alienated and enemies in your mind by wicked works, yet now hath he reconciled. In the body of his flesh through death, to present you holy and unblameable and unreproveable in his sight."

It will be readily understood that the great apostle in this wonderful tribute, knew that he was not writing about the son of Jospeh, the carpenter, but the virgin-born Son of God, the pre-existent Christ, the Creator of all things. It were folly to try to rob the beloved disciple John and the great Apostle Paul of their belief in the incarnated, virgin-born Son of God who had existed from the eternities. In order to reveal the will of God, his love for fallen men and his power to save them from sin, he manifested himself in the flesh, suffered and died upon the cross, arose from the dead and ascended into heaven.

If Jesus had the high character, and was the being described by the brilliant skeptics from whom we have quoted in the earlier part of this discourse, his statements with reference to himself should be received at their face value as absolute proof. Jesus could not be what Lecky, Renan and Mill said he was, what the inspired apostle claimed for him, and yet be a boastful deceiver, making false claims for himself.

We shall now consider the claims Jesus Christ made for himself. Being the great character model and supreme teacher that agnostics and skeptics admit Christ to be, is it too much to suppose that Jesus understood and knew himself and his unique place among men? Shall we grant that, he of all teachers, knew most about men, their needs and the conduct which would secure for them the greatest good in life, and yet did not know himself? Was this man of spotless character, this teacher of the highest truth, a mere pretender, when he said to the paralytic let down through the roof, "Son, thy sins be forgiven thee?" Was he a boastful mesmerist when he said, "That ye may know that the Son of man hath power on earth to forgive sins, I say unto thee (the paralytic) Arise, take up thy bed and go unto thine house."

The same disciple who gives a record of the wonderful claims of Christ tells us the sick man was healed at once, to the amazement of the bystanders. By what sort of mental gymnastics does your modern skeptic summersault over the record of the miracles of Christ, and his claim to have power to forgive sins, as fiction or forgery, and yet, accept his teachings as the sanest philosophy and highest wisdom.

Christ could have made no higher claim, be he man or God incarnate, than that he could forgive sins. If he was only a man the claim was blasphemous, his teaching false, his character vile. If he was God manifest in the flesh, as he claimed to be, his character is spotless, his teachings absolute truth; he could, he did, and he can, forgive sins. In either event, the teachings of the agnostic and modernist are illogical, irreverent, unscriptural, false and destructive to saving faith.

Jesus not only claimed to have power to forgive sins, but he claimed to have power to raise the dead. Note his words as he approached the grave of his dead friend, Lazarus: "I am the resurrection, and the life: he that believeth in me, though he were dead, yet shall he live; and whosoever liveth and believeth in me shall never die."

The record of this remarkable declaration of Christ tells us he immediately demonstrated the truth of his claim by raising Lazarus from the dead. Could the God of the universe have made a higher claim than Jesus makes here? We have it here in the record, claiming to be inspired truth. What shall we do with it? Shall we have the daring audacity to claim that the great Teacher spoke the truth when speaking of men and things pertaining to individuals and society, but spoke a falsehood when speaking of himself?

It appears to me, that any sort of consistency demands that we declare Jesus to be a boastful, blasphemous, fanatical pretender of the most deceptive and dangerous character, or we must accept his claim to be the Son of God manifest in the flesh, and clothed with all the supernatural powers he claimed to possess and exercise.

Your modernistic preachers who deny the virgin birth of Christ, therefore his Godhead, who deny that he performed miracles, therefore, making him only a man, with no redeeming power in himself, dare not, as yet, hold him up as a fanatical pretender; even the blatant, intelligent infidel does not go so

far as this.   But what about this claim
of Christ to raise the dead, if he was
only a man, even the best man that ever
lived.   Such a claim as this was utterly
false, deceptive and misleading on the
most serious and important subject
that can claim the attention of immor-
tal beings. Mr. Fosdick, the high priest
of modern liberalists, and the lean theo-
logians and shallow philosophers who
follow him with such noisy applause,
should take time to think these things
through.   Invincible logic and common
honesty must compel them to accept
Jesus Christ the Son of God, as Saviour
and Lord, or reject him as one of the
most daring deceivers who has ever ap-
peared among men.

Let us gather up some of the "I ams"
of Jesus and give them the consideration of reasonable beings.   "I am the
bread of life."   John 6:48.   "I am the
light of the world."   John 8:12.   "Before Abraham was, I am."   John 8:56.
"I am from above: Ye are of this world.
I am not of this world."   John 8:23.
"I am the resurrection, and the life."
John 11:25.   "I am the way, the truth,
and the life; no man cometh to the
Father but by me."   John 14:6.

It would seem that modern liberalists, agnostics and skeptics of every class would admit that if God, in the solution of the sin problem, and the saving and uplift of the race, has chosen to incarnate himself and come into the world in the form of a man, he could not have made higher claims for himself than the claims which Jesus made for himself. They were either true or false. If they were true, every phase of unbelief in Christ is false and destructive of the peace and happiness of mankind here and hereafter. If these statements of Jesus were false, the Christian Church has no right to exist and ought to perish and disappear from the earth.

The great Napoleon once remarked: "It is true that Christ proposes to our faith a series of mysteries. He commands with authority, that we should believe them, giving no other reason than those tremendous words, 'I am God.' He declares it! What an abyss he creates by that declaration between himself and all the fabrications of religion. What audacity! What sacrilege! What blasphemy, if it were not true!" The logic of the great soldier is sound. Jesus was, and is, what he claimed to be, or he practiced diabolical deception. He was not a deceiver, but the Son of God, the only and all-sufficient Saviour of men. Let us look furthre into the claims Jesus made for himself. We shall call attention to only two of these high claims: We have in our Lord's words to Philip the very highest claim he could possibly make for himself. "Philip saith unto him, Lord, show us the Father, and it sufficeth us." "Jesus saith unto him, have I been so long time with you, and yet hast thou not known me, Philip? He that hath seen me hath seen the Father; and how sayest thou then, show us the Father?"

Could the faultless man offered us by skeptics and philosophers make such a claim as we have here, and remain faultless? These men are utterly illogical. Christ was what he claimed to be, or he was a blasphemer. Who would dare to insinuate that he was a blasphemer, except those blinded priests who sentenced him to death because he claimed to be the Son of God, and one with the eternal Father; and those modernists who join themselves with this Sanhedrin who denied his Godhead, and sent him to the Roman cross.

We will give in conclusion of this

phase of the subject one of the very high claims made by our blessed Lord, found in Matthew 11:28, 29. It reads, "Come unto me, all ye that labor and are heavy laden, and I will give you rest. Take my yoke upon you, and learn of me; for I am meek and lowly in heart: and ye shall find rest unto your souls." Here our Lord is offering his omnipotent shoulders to bear the burdens of all the races crushed beneath the weight of sin and sorrow, of ignorance, poverty, sickness and distress. He calls every burdened soul in all the wide realm of human habitation to come to him with the absolute promise that they shall have rest. This is not the promise of a mere man; it is the gracious offer of God manifest in the flesh, of One who, through the centuries, has demonstrated himself able to lift the burden of sin and sorrow, and to give rest to every penitent soul that has come to him with faith in his deity and the atonement he has made upon the cross.

There is a vast background connected with the Christ before his appearance in physical form in the world, which we have not time to enter now. If we should, we could find that there is a vast realm of prophecy foretelling his coming, his character, his teaching, his suffering, his victory over the grave, the spread of his gospel, the growth of his kingdom, and his final triumphant and glorious reign over mankind.

We could find in the building of the temple, and the offering of the various sacrifices, that the Lord and Saviour was typified and foretold in the death of innocent and sinless victims for the guilt of wicked men. Every innocent lamb slain and burned upon a Hebrew altar was pointing to the Lamb of God who was to come and take away the sin of the world.

We have not time nor space to "Let the redeemed say so." But for almost two thousand years untold millions, by simple faith, have been able to demonstrate the fact that Jesus Christ is the Son of God, and that he has power on earth to forgive sins; that he can, and does, give rest to weary, sin-burdened souls; that he has fulfilled the gracious promise that, "Whosoever cometh unto me I will in no wise cast out."

Our Lord Jesus has promised that the Father would send the Comforter, even the Spirit of truth, whom the world, the unregenerated, could not receive. This divine Comforter can take

the things of Christ and reveal them
unto us. Jesus says of this Comforter,
"He shall testify of me." The Holy
Spirit has power to reveal Christ to the
individual in such way that the trust-
ing heart has a full assurance beyond
the possibility of question or doubt.

Jesus had this gracious fact in mind
when he said to Peter, on his good con-
fession that Christ was the Son of the
living God, "Flesh and blood hath not
revealed this unto thee, but my Father." We have the full promise that the
Holy Spirit will give us such revela-
tions of Christ that he shall be to us as
real a person as he was to his disciples
when he walked and talked with men.
Here we have in John 14:21, a most
gracious promise: "He that hath my
commandments, and keepeth them, he
it is that loveth me: and he that loveth
me shall be loved of my Father, and I
will love him, and will manifest myself
to him." The blessed manifestation
that Jesus can, and does, give of himself to those who have sought and found
in him a Saviour from sin, establishes
and confirms them in a faith that will
not, cannot, shrink, though pressed by
every foe.

This whole question of the Virgin

Birth, Godhead, sacrificial death and bodily resurrection of our Lord is most vital. We can make no surrender or compromise here, and at the same time, retain and preach a saving gospel. The Christ of the Bible, as revealed in the prophecies of the Old Testament and in the gospels and epistles of the New Testament, is the Son of God, the only and all-sufficient Saviour of mankind.

"All hail the power of Jesus' name!
  Let angels prostrate fall;
Bring forth the royal diadem
  And crown him Lord of all!"

Let every burdened, sinful soul come to Jesus. Do not hesitate. He came to seek and to save. However far you may have wandered in your prodigality, or deeply you have sinned, he can, and will, forgive. He will sanctify and cleanse. He is able and willing to meet all the needs of all human beings. All he asks is, that we come to him with surrendered hearts and simple trust that appropriates the full provision he has made for our salvation. Come to Christ, and come NOW!

www.ingramcontent.com/pod-product-compliance
Lightning Source LLC
Chambersburg PA
CBHW030009040426
42337CB00012BA/710